D1048021

Home Is
Where Your Mom Is

Spiritual Thoughts for Mothers

JAMES W. MOORE

Abingdon Press

NASHVILLE

Home Is
Where Your Mom Is

Library of Congress Cataloging-in-Publication Data has been requested.

ISBN 978-1-4267-6798-2

All scripture quotations unless noted otherwise are taken from the New Revised Standard Version of the Bible, copyright 1989, Division of Christian Education of the National Council of the Churches of Christ in the United States of America. Used by permission. All rights reserved.

Scripture quotations marked (NIV) are taken from the Holy Bible, New International Version®, NIV®. Copyright © 1973, 1978, 1984, 2011 by Biblica, Inc.™ Used by permission of Zondervan. All rights reserved worldwide. www.zondervan.com. The "NIV" and "New International Version" are trademarks registered in the United States Patent and Trademark Office by Biblica, Inc.™

13 14 15 16 17 18 19 20 21 22—10 9 8 7 6 5 4 3 2 1

MANUFACTURED IN THE UNITED STATES OF AMERICA

CONTENTS

INTRODUCTION

IT'S BECAUSE
SHE'S A MOTHER

Mark 7:24-30

Let me begin by stringing together three illustrations. See if you can find the common thread that links them together.

ILLUSTRATION NUMBER ONE

His name was Mel. He was reflecting about his mom and how she had brought him up, and he said these words:

You know, my granddaughters talk now about needing their privacy and how they have a right to keep secrets in their room. Maybe so, but I sure didn't have that right. My mom used to go in my room daily, and I know she pulled out every drawer in my dresser to see if I was up to anything she didn't like.

In those times ... parents kept up better on what was going on with their kids. I don't know that they loved their children more than parents do now, but they did seem to stay better informed. ... If something was wrong they knew it when I walked in the door.

ILLUSTRATION NUMBER TWO

I received an e-mail last May, just a few days before Mother's Day, with the poem "The Meanest Mother in the World."

I had the meanest mother in the world!

While other kids ate candy for breakfast, I had to have cereal, eggs and toast. When others had Coke and candy for lunch, I had to eat a sandwich. As you can guess, my dinner was different from other kids' too.

My mother insisted on knowing where we were all the time. You'd think we were on a chain gang. She had to know who our friends were and what we were doing. . . .

I am ashamed to admit it, but she actually had the nerve to break the child labor law—she made us work. We had to wash dishes, make beds, learn to cook, and all sorts of odd things. I believe she lay awake nights thinking of mean things to do to us. She always insisted on us telling the truth, the whole truth and nothing but the truth.

By the time we were teenagers, she was much wiser, and our lives at home became even more unbearable. None of this tooting the car horn for us to come running. She embarrassed us to no end by making our friends and dates come to the door to get us.

I forgot to mention that while my friends were dating at the mature age of twelve or thirteen, my old-fashioned mother refused to let me date until I was fifteen or sixteen. She even made us go to church with her and dad.

My mother was a complete failure as a mother. None of us

has ever been arrested. Each of my five brothers has served in the military service of this country. And who do we have to thank for this terrible way we turned out? You're right. Our mean mother!

Look at all the things we missed.... She made us grow up into God-fearing, educated, honest adults. I am trying to raise my children and stand a little taller, and I am filled with pride when my children call me mean.

You see, thank God, he gave me the meanest mother in the world—from this I would say the country doesn't need a good 5 cent cigar, it needs more mean mothers and dads.

ILLUSTRATION NUMBER THREE

This powerful story came out of the French Revolution. A mother had wandered through the woods for three days with her two children, trying to survive on roots and leaves.

On the third day, she heard soldiers approaching, so quickly she hid herself and her children behind some bushes. The sergeant in charge heard a noise. He prodded the bushes to see what was stirring behind them. When he saw the starving woman and the two children, he gave them a loaf of brown bread.

The mother took it eagerly, broke it into two pieces, and gave one piece to each child. "She has kept none for herself," the sergeant said.

"Is it because she is not hungry?" a young soldier asked.

"No," said the sergeant, "it's because she is a Mother."

The common thread through all of these stories is obvious. They are all about the love of a mother and how that love can be expressed in a variety of ways.

Mother's Day comes around once each year to remind us of how important it is to have solid homes and strong families. A Spanish proverb expresses it wonderfully: "An ounce of mother is worth a pound of clergy." A Middle Eastern proverb says: "A child without a mother is like a door without a knob." And one Mother's Day, a minister paid his mother this perfect tribute: "My mother practices what I preach."

All of these are great sayings about the dramatic importance of motherhood, but one of my favorites is the title of this book: "Home Is Where Your Mom Is."

A MOTHER'S LOVE

Mark:7:24-30

There was a McDonald's commercial that depicted a young executive coming home from work in a bad mood. He loosened his tie, dropped his briefcase on the floor, slumped into his easy chair, and said: "This has been a horrible day." Then his son (eight or nine years old) walked in, slumped on the couch, and said, "You think your day was bad, you should hear about mine." The dad said, "My most important client was impossible." The boy said, "My math teacher surprised us with a pop quiz." The dad said, "And on the way home, my car broke down." The boy said, "Well, on the way home, my bike broke down." Just then the wife and mother walked into the room and said, "Sounds like I need to take you boys to McDonald's." Then the camera came in close on the little boy, and he said: "That's why I love that woman!"

What was that little boy talking about? What was it that prompted that kind of love for his mother? It was her love that didn't wait to be asked, her love that saw the need and met it, her "Godlike love" that reached out with grace.

I like that commercial because it's funny, but even more because it reminds us dramatically about the power we have to influence others in our homes. And who has more power to influence others than a devoted, loving, faithful mother! There are a lot of important jobs in the world today but not one of them is more important than the job of being a mother. After all, who has a better opportunity to shape and influence young lives than a mother?

So, with that in mind, let me share something with you that I discovered recently. It's called "Somebody Said," and it includes these words:

• Somebody said it takes about six weeks to get back to normal after you've had a baby... Somebody doesn't know that once you're a mother, "normal" is history. Somebody said you learn how to be a mother by instinct... Somebody never took a three-year-old shopping. Somebody said being a mother is boring... Somebody never rode in a car driven by a teenager with a driver's permit. Somebody said you don't need an education to be a mother... Somebody never helped a fourth grader with her math. Somebody said you can't love the fifth child as much as you love the first... Somebody doesn't have five children. Somebody said the hardest part of being a mother is labor and delivery... Somebody never watched her "baby" get on the bus for the first day of kindergarten or on a plane headed for military boot camp. Somebody said your mother knows you love her, so you don't need to tell her... Somebody isn't a mother.

The common thread that runs through all of these sayings is obvious. They are all about the love of a mother and how that love can be expressed in words, attitudes, and actions.

That is precisely what we see in the scripture for this chapter in Mark 7 as this Greek mother comes to Jesus for help. Her daughter is sick, she has heard about Jesus and his power to heal. So, as a loving, concerned mom, she comes to Jesus. She kneels before him and asks him to heal her daughter.

At first glance, it seems as though Jesus is being a bit harsh with the Greek woman because he says: "Let the children be fed first, for it is not fair to take the children's bread and throw it to the dogs" (v. 27).

What in the world does that mean?

Well, the word *children* refers to the Jews, and the word *dogs* refers to the Gentiles. The Jews regarded the Gentiles as "unclean," and their most notorious term of contempt for the Gentiles was "dogs," the wild, filthy, flea-bitten dogs of the street.

But interestingly, Jesus does not use that word. In the original Greek text, he does not use the word that refers to the dirty street dogs. Rather, he uses the diminutive word, which refers to the little pet dogs of the house, the family's beloved puppies.

When he did that, the Greek woman realized immediately that he was speaking with a smile, and that she was with a friend, and that help was on the way. The woman was a Greek, and the Greeks had a great love for conversation, dialogue, and friendly debate. They loved banter, repartee, mental sparring. Not only that, but back then men did not discuss theological issues with women. Women back then were treated as inferior, as mindless, as things to be owned and discarded.

But Jesus honors her by including her in a philosophical, theological discussion, the kind that was so important in the Greek world of old. Because of this, the Greek woman understands that Jesus is befriending her, and she skillfully rises to the occasion with a brilliant response. She says: Yes, I know the children are fed first, but surely, I can have the crumbs under the table, which the children have thrown away.

Jesus loved her response. He liked her spirit. Hers was a sunny faith that would not quit, a persistent faith that would not take no for an answer. Here was a mother with a sick child at home who was willing to take a chance for the sake of her child.

When tested, she responded with grace and grit,

with charm and insight. And Jesus was impressed. He liked her. He liked her boldness and her commitment to her child. And he answered her prayer. "For saying that," he said to her, "you may go—the demon has left your daughter" (v. 29).

The Greek woman returned home quickly and found that indeed her mission had been accomplished. Just as Jesus had said, her daughter was completely healed. The illness was totally gone. He had, indeed, made her well!

This is a fascinating story, and at this point, we could go in a number of different directions. We could look at the power of Jesus to heal, the effect of the woman's bold persistence, or the Greek woman as a symbol of all the Gentiles and their inclusion in God's kingdom. But for now, let me invite you to look with me at the poignant portrait of love painted here. In this Greek mother's encounter with Jesus, we see three of the most important ways to express love.

WE CAN EXPRESS LOVE WITH WORDS

Love can be expressed with words. The Greek woman came to Jesus that day to express in words her love for her sick child. Also, in the Gospel of Mark, she is the only person who lovingly calls Jesus "Lord."

It seems as though it would be so easy to express our love with words, but the truth is that precious few people do that well. Why is that? Why do we have trouble speaking the words of love? If we only realized how powerful words are, I think we would work harder at the task of expressing our love with words.

Some years ago, a woman was dying in a local hospital. She was in her mid-eighties. Her son flew in to be with her. I happened to be present when he entered the room. He walked over to the bedside of his dying mother. He leaned over and kissed her on the cheek. Then, touched by that tender moment of seeing her so weak and vulnerable and dying, he said to her: "Mom, you have been such a good mother to me. And, I want you to know I love you."

And, through tears, she said: "Son, that's the first time you've ever told me. Last Friday was your sixty-third birthday, and that's the first time you ever told me." Isn't that something? It took him sixty-three years to say "I love you" to his mother.

Let me ask you something. Is there a word of love

you need to speak today? For those of you fortunate enough to still have your parents, how long has it been since you told your mom or dad how much you love them and appreciate them? How long has it been since you told your mate? I don't mean a quick, routine, matter-of-fact "I love you," but a real heart-to-heart expression of your love in words.

And mothers, how about you? How long has it been since you told your children how proud you are of them and how much you cherish them? Let me suggest something. For one week, write down every word you say to your children and then ask: *How many of these words are words of love, encouragement and appreciation and not just words of correction or discipline?* I know as parents we have to be referees sometimes, and that is a loving thing to do, but also we need to be cheerleaders. We need to say "I love you."

There is no question about it. One of the best ways to express love is with words.

WE CAN EXPRESS LOVE WITH ATTITUDE

We can express our love with our attitude toward life. One of the things about the Greek woman that impressed Jesus most was her attitude. She was committed to her child, and she was willing to do whatever it took to get help for her sick daughter.

She was bold, determined, persistent, and courageous because she lived by the attitude of love. She would not be discouraged. She would not give up, because she lived by the attitude of love.

Some years ago in a mining town in West Virginia, a seventeen-year-old boy took a summer job in the coal mines. Being a "coal miner for the summer" sounded adventuresome and macho.

However, the second week on the job, he got lost deep down in the mines. He had been working with a group of veteran miners. They had warned him. They had cautioned him. They had told him to stay close to the group because it would be so easy to get lost down there in the numerous caves and treacherous passageways of the mine.

But he was seventeen years old. One day he, absentmindedly wandered away from his work team, and he became lost—completely lost! He screamed for help, but the miners had moved on to another location, and no one could hear him.

Then, suddenly, his light went out, and he was in total darkness. He was absolutely terrified. He began to cry. He thought to himself, *This is how it all ends for me. I'm going to die down here. I don't know which way to go. I don't know how to get out.* He dropped down on his knees to pray: "O, God, help me!" he said out loud. "O, God, please help me!"

Then he noticed something. As he was kneeling there to pray, he felt his right knee touching something hard. He felt it. It was a railroad track. He realized that if he kept his hand on that track and followed it, it would lead him out! So he held onto the track, and eventually, it brought him out of the dark, out of the depths of the mine to light and safety.

That's a parable for us, isn't it? If we will hold onto the track of love and follow wherever it leads, if we will make love our attitude in life, no matter how dark some moments may be, the love-track will bring us out and lead us to the light.

As "cliché-ish" as it may sound, it is still profoundly true: Love is the answer, so we would do well to hold onto that track and to live by that attitude. As

Christians, that is our calling: to live always by the spirit and attitude of love. We can express our love with words and with attitude.

WE CAN EXPRESS LOVE WITH ACTIONS

That Greek mother in Mark 7 put her love to work. She acted it out. She expressed her love with actions. How important that is!

I went to college with a girl from Sarawak, Borneo. Her grandfather had been a headhunter. When she was in high school, she went one night to a youth program led by a Methodist college student. That night she was converted. She accepted Christ as her Savior and dedicated her life to him.

But then she had a problem. How would she tell her parents about her newfound faith? She decided not to tell them in words but rather to show them in deeds of love She explained:

> Before Christ came into my life, I was spoiled and selfish. I was irritable and impatient. I was disrespectful to my parents. My room was a mess and my attitude was worse. But

after Christ came into my life, I changed. I was kind to my parents. I cleaned up my room. I helped with the housework. I spoke with tenderness and respect to my parents. I was loving toward everyone.

My parents noticed and they said to me: "You are different! Why? What has happened to you?"

I said, "Yes, I am different because I have been reborn! I have Christ as my Savior. I am a Christian now and Christians always live by the law of love."

And her parents said: "Tell us more of this religion. Tell us more of this Christ. If he can change people like that, we want to be Christians, too!"

Well, that's the way it works. We can express our love with words, with attitude, but most powerfully, most dramatically, most meaningfully with actions!

T W O

JESUS INCREASED IN WISDOM AND STATURE AND IN FAVOR WITH GOD AND PEOPLE

Luke 2:52

Two paddleboats left Memphis about the same time, heading down the Mississippi to New Orleans. As they traveled side by side, some sailors from one of the boats began to make derogatory remarks about the slow pace of the other boat. Words were exchanged. Insults were shouted. Challenges were made.

And the race began. Competition became vicious as the two boats roared through the Deep South.

One boat began falling behind. Not enough fuel. There had been plenty of coal for the normal trip, but not nearly enough for a fast and furious race. As the boat dropped back, an enterprising and overly competitive young sailor grabbed some of the ship's cargo and tossed it into the boat's furnace. When the other sailors on his boat saw what the young sailor was doing, and when they realized that the supplies burned as well as the coal, they got excited!

They quickly fueled their boat with the cargo they had been assigned to transport. They ended up winning the race, but in the process, they burned up and lost all of their precious cargo!

There is a sermon there somewhere because, you see, God has entrusted to us some special and precious cargo: our children, our grandchildren, our spouses, our friends, our neighbors, our church, and our own souls. Our job is to do our part in seeing that this cargo entrusted to us reaches its intended destination.

But when the rush to success becomes so furious and takes priority over people (especially the family), then people suffer, people get hurt. Think of it. How much precious cargo do we sacrifice in order to achieve the number-one slot? How many people never reach their destination because of the aggressiveness and the mixed-up priorities of a competitive captain?

Jesus warned us about this. He said, "For what will it profit them to gain the whole world and forfeit their life?" (Mark 8:36). What does it profit to win the rat race and lose your precious cargo in the process?

The point is clear. We must get back to emphasizing and cultivating the Christian home. It is urgent that we make the Christian home a top priority. Whether that home has nine people in it or one person in it, it is crucial that Christian faith and Christian virtues and Christian values are lived out there. The Christian home should be the very first place we learn to celebrate life as a precious gift from God, where we learn to love and we are loved unconditionally. The Christian home should be the very first place we learn the difference between right and wrong, the first place we learn how to share and to respect others. The Christian home should be the very first place we learn how to pray and to hear the stories of Jesus.

Go to any prison today and interview the prisoners about how they ended up behind bars. You will find that the vast majority of them will tell you that they came from dysfunctional families, that their problems trace back to a bad situation at home, a destructive family. Let me hurry to say: not all of them! I personally know some situations where the parents did everything right and still their child got into trouble. But most of the time, the prisoners will say their problems trace back to their early home life.

So the lesson for us is obvious. In the home:

- Build your child's self-esteem.
- Emphasize self-worth and self-respect.
- Teach your children independent and wise decision-making.
- Remind them constantly that they are special to you and special to God.
- Teach them the Christian faith, but more important, live your faith before them.
- Keep them close to church and Sunday school and youth fellowship.
- Teach them the scriptures.

- Teach them to pray, but even better, let them see and hear you pray.
- Make them dramatically aware of how much you and God and the church love them.
- And most important, introduce them to Jesus Christ! Tell them the stories of Jesus, and let them see the spirit of Jesus Christ in you.

The last verse of the second chapter of Luke's gospel is fascinating. Earlier in this chapter, Luke told the story of Jesus' birth, his presentation in the Temple as a child, and the story of how Jesus as a young boy was left behind in Jerusalem accidentally and was found three days later by his parents. He was in the Temple sitting and discussing theology with the scribes and elders. And then, Luke concludes chapter 2 with this sentence: "Jesus matured in wisdom and years, and in favor with God and people" (CEB). That is, he grew in mind, body, and spirit.

When a Tennessee woman celebrated her ninety-eighth birthday, someone asked what was her formula for such a long, happy, healthy, and productive life. She said, "Three things: think good thoughts, be kind to everybody, and eat prunes every day." Now, what she was saying was, she had taken care of her mind, her body, and her soul. That's our calling in the Christian home and the Christian church: to help children of all ages grow in mind, body, and spirit—to increase in wisdom and stature, and in favor with God and people. Let's take a look at each of these.

WE HELP OUR CHILDREN GROW IN WISDOM (IN MIND)

It's important to recognize that *book knowledge* and *wisdom* are not the same. I have known in my lifetime some people who were well educated and also very wise, but I have also known people who had no formal education at all and yet were also amazingly wise.

Wisdom is not knowing all the answers on *Jeopardy* or getting all the answers right on the final exam. According to the Bible, wisdom is the ability to know and understand God's will and the grace to do it. And you know, that's really what it means today, isn't it? And that's the crucial thing we need to teach our children at home and in church.

Some years ago, a preacher told about something

in his youth. He said before he came into the ministry that he had a great and vast experience in the theater. He said he had swept the floors, popped the popcorn, and sold the tickets, and that was the extent of his great experience in the theater.

He also said that as he worked in the theater in his hometown, they typically showed those old Western movies. The actors were different and the horses were different, but the story was the same every Saturday. It was the good guys against the outlaws, and in the end, right would prevail and the good guys in the white hats would always win.

He went on to say that the one cowboy in those movies that he liked the most, the one he wanted to grow up to be like most of all, was the guy who rode out into the desert, got off his horse, knelt down, and put his hand and ear to the ground and said, "Two men approaching on horseback . . . riding out of the mountains, wearing six-shooters . . . and carrying a rifle." The preacher said he admired that guy (the guide, the tracker) because he was always so cool and confident and composed. He was always so wise.

One Saturday it would be John Wayne, and the

next Saturday Gary Cooper or Randolph Scott or Roy Rogers or Gene Autry. Whichever one it was, he was always so wise. He always knew what was coming, and he always knew just what to do to save the day. He was the tracker, the leader, the guide.

Don't you wish we had a guide like that today? Someone who could show us just the right thing to do the wise thing to do? Well, as a matter of fact, we have an even better tracker and leader and guide: his name is Jesus. He is the way, the truth, and the life. He is the Word of God, the Purpose of God, the Wisdom of God, wrapped up in a living person.

Some years ago, there was a great professor at Centenary College named Dean R. E. Smith. Dean Smith was a saintly man, a brilliant scholar, an outstanding communicator, and a real friend to the students. In one of his most famous lectures, Dean Smith would talk to the students about how we discover truth, how we determine what is true and what is false.

After some discussion, Dean Smith would suddenly ask the students, "How wide is my desk?" The students would look at the large desk and then make their best guesses. A variety of answers would ring out.

"I think it's about 72 inches wide." "No, I believe it's more like 68 inches wide." "Looks like 75 to me." Then some wise guy from the back of the room would say, "71 5/16," and everybody would laugh. Then Dean Smith would say, "These are all pretty good guesses, but how do we figure out which one is most nearly true and accurate?" There would be silence in the classroom for a moment, and then tentatively someone would say, "Get a measuring stick?" "That's right," Dean Smith would say. "To determine which answer is closest to the truth, we have to get a measuring stick and measure."

Then Dean Smith would go to the blackboard, take a piece of chalk, and in silence he would draw the outline of a cross. He would trace over and over the sign of the cross, letting it dramatically sink into the hearts and minds of those students. Then, he would stand back and point to that cross and say, "Ladies and gentlemen, there's your measuring stick! There's your measuring stick for truth!"

Now, look with me at that cross. There's our compass, our tracker, our guide. There's our measuring stick for truth. We can put our confidence in that. If the world tells you that it's OK to take advantage of others for your own personal gain; if the world tries to tell you that it's not so bad to lie or cheat or hurt or steal or hold a grudge or hate, you just remember the cross. Remember the truth of Christ.

The measuring stick of Christ tells us to be committed to God and compassionate toward one another; to be loving and caring and kind; to be just and honest and truthful; to be loyal and merciful and gracious. Anything that doesn't measure up to that is wrong and destructive and sinful! That's what we need to teach our children: to let Jesus Christ and his cross be the measuring stick for what is right and good and true. That's number one: we help our children grow in wisdom.

WE HELP OUR CHILDREN GROW IN STATURE (IN BODY)

Of course, in Luke 2 as we read that "Jesus increased in stature," it means that his body developed. He became taller and stronger. But also in the Bible the word *body* often means more than our physical makeup. Quite often it means "total personality" and sometimes even now the word *stature* means character.

For example, if you hear a woman described as "a person of great stature in her community," you don't think physically about that. You don't think the woman is seven feet tall and weighs three hundred pounds. No, you think that she is a person noted and respected for her strength of character and influence and morality. It is so crucial that we teach our children the importance of honesty and integrity and ethical living.

USA TODAY once had a large article on two cowboy churches in Texas. They printed the Cowboy's Ten Commandments. The writer of the *USA TODAY* article found the Cowboy's Ten Commandments posted on the wall at Cross Trails Church in Fairlie, Texas. The cowboys said they and their children could understand this version of the Ten Commandments better than the one with the "thou shalt not"s in it, and they said they could live up to them a lot better. The meaning is the same but the words are "down home Texas."

1. Just one God.

2. Honor yer Ma and Pa.

3. No telling tales or gossipin'.

4. Git yourself to Sunday meeting.

5. Put nothin' before God.

6. No foolin' around with another fellow's gal.

7. No killin'.

8. Watch yer mouth.

9. Don't take what ain't yers.

10. Don't be hankerin' for yer buddy's stuff.

In Texas cowboys just tell it like it is, but however we tell it, we need to go to bed at night and get up in the morning and all in between teaching our children what's right and what's wrong, what's good and what's bad, what's just and what's unjust.

First, we help our children grown in wisdom, and second, we help our children grown in stature.

WE HELP OUR CHILDREN GROW IN FAVOR WITH GOD AND PEOPLE (IN SPIRIT, IN SOUL, IN RELATIONSHIPS)

Some years ago, a famous actor was touring the country doing a one-man show in small towns to promote drama and the fine arts. One evening he came to a small village and everyone in town came out to see him and hear him. He was masterful and at the end of his performance there was a thunderous standing ovation. He had performed selections from Broadway, Shakespeare, movies, and history, and the people were mesmerized by his incredible talent.

They applauded and cheered, and he came back on stage for an encore. He quieted the crowd and asked for requests. Seated on the front row was an older man who had been the pastor in that small village for many years. The people all loved the elderly minister, and they all turned to him to see if he wanted to request something for the famous actor to do. The old pastor said, "I have a favorite, but our honored guest may not know it."

"What is it?" the actor asked.

The elderly minister said, "The 23rd Psalm, the Shepherd's Psalm."

The actor said, "I know it well and I'll be glad to do it on one condition—that after I recite it, the minister will come and recite it too."

At first the old minister tried to decline, saying he didn't feel worthy to be on the same stage with this world-famous actor. But the actor insisted, and the crowd called out for the minister to do it. So finally, but reluctantly, he gave in and went up on stage.

The actor went first. He recited the 23rd Psalm with breathtaking eloquence and when he finished, there was a five-minute standing ovation. The older minister stood there in silence for a moment, thinking, *How in the world could I follow that?* But then he started thinking about how over the years God had been his Shepherd, and he began to quote the beautiful Shepherd's Psalm. "The Lord is my Shepherd, I shall not want..." and when he finished there was no applause—just holy and reverent silence. It was so powerful that tears filled the eyes of everyone in the auditorium. The actor walked over and put his arm around the shoulders of the old minister and said to the audience, "My friends, did you notice that there was a difference in the way the two of us recited the 23rd Psalm?" The actor paused for a moment and then he said, "The difference was this: I know the Shepherd's Psalm, but he knows the Shepherd!"

Do you know the Shepherd? Do you know him, really? Do your children know him? It is so important, so crucial, so urgent to help our children grow in mind, body, and spirit; to grow in wisdom and in stature and in favor with God and people.

THREE

THIS LITTLE LIGHT OF MINE, I'M GONNA LET IT SHINE

Matthew 5:14-17

Recently, I ran across a list of imagined Mothers' cautions from history. Take a look at some of these:

1. Paul Revere's mother: "I don't care where you think you have to go, young man. Midnight is past your curfew.

2. Mona Lisa's mother: "After all that money your father and I spent on braces, Mona, that's the biggest smile you can give us?"

3. Columbus's mother: "I don't care what you've discovered, Christopher, you still could have written!"

4. Michelangelo's mother: "Look, Mikey, why can't you paint on the walls like other children? Do you have any idea how hard it is to get that stuff off the ceiling?"

5. Abraham Lincoln's mother: "Again with the stovepipe hat, Abe? Why can't you wear a baseball cap like the other kids?"

6. Albert Einstein's mother: "But, Albert, it's your senior picture. Can't you do something about your hair? Styling gel, mousse, something?"

7. Jonah's mother: "That's a nice story, Jonah, but now tell me where you've really been for the last three days."

8. Thomas Edison's mother: "Of course I'm proud that you invented the light bulb, Thomas. Now, turn off that light and get to bed!"

Well, in the Sermon on the Mount, Jesus told us to turn on the light of Christian influence. He said it like this:

You are the light of the world … (So), let your light so shine before others, so that they may see your good works and give glory to your Father in heaven. (Matthew 5:14-16)

The famous spiritual expresses it like this:

This little light of mine,

I'm gonna let it shine.

Let it shine, let it shine, let it shine.

The words of Jesus and the words of the spiritual are underscoring how dramatically important it is that we let the light of Christ shine through us, that we exert Christian influence in the world.

Albert Schweitzer has had a great and powerful Christian influence on the world. I love what Norman Cousins said about him: "The greatness of Schweitzer … is not so much what he has done for others, but what others have done because of him and the power of his example. This is the measure of the man" (*The Saturday Review*, 1954).

Isn't that a great quote? *It's not so much what he has done, but what others have done because of him.*

Isn't that the real measure of every person? It's not just what we do, but it's what we cause others to do. It's what others do because of us. It's the power of our example, the weight of our influence.

Be honest now: how do you measure up? What kind of example are you? How do you influence other people? What do others do because of you? How brightly does the light of Christ shine in you?

Some years ago, a group of educators in our country wanted to honor Albert Schweitzer, and they brought him to America. The University of Chicago planned to give him an honorary degree. Dr. McGifford of the university went with a group to meet Schweitzer's train. They saw Albert Schweitzer get off the train. They greeted him, welcomed him warmly, and told him of their joy in having him there. But then as they turned to leave the train station, suddenly Schweitzer was gone. He just disappeared, vanished, slipped away. They looked everywhere for him. When they found him, guess what he was doing. He was carrying a suitcase for an elderly woman.

You see, it was so much a part of his life—his Christ-inspired life—that it was just the natural thing for him when he got off the train to begin immediately to look for somebody he could help.

But the thing I remember most about that story was what Dr. McGifford said later when he reflected on it. He said, "When I saw Dr. Schweitzer helping that woman with her suitcase, I was wishing like everything that I could find somebody whose suitcase I could carry." The power of influence, the power of example. It's not just what you do, it's what others do because of you. Schweitzer is an example of a Christian man who made those around him want to do good.

But of course, the perfect example of this was Jesus. It wasn't just what he did, it was also what he caused others to do. It was the power of his influence. Think of the lives he touched, the lives he changed, the lives he saved. To some he gave new sight, new vision. To some, he gave a new start. To some, he gave a new confidence. To some, he gave wholeness.

Think of it: the power of his influence. Because of his influence

- The impetuous and vacillating Simon Peter became a rock.

- The woman of the streets, Mary Magdalene, became instead a woman of faith.
- The self-seeking James who had dreams of prestige and power and position later became one of the first to give his life for the Christian faith.
- A small band of disciples, just as different as they could be—a motley crew with no money, no political power, no military weapons—turned the world upside down because of the influence Jesus had upon them.

It wasn't just what Jesus did; it was what others did because of him. James Francis expressed it beautifully in that classic piece, *One Solitary Life*.

He was born in an obscure village, the child of a peasant woman. He grew up in still another village where He worked in a carpenter shop until He was thirty, and then for three years He was an itinerant preacher. He never wrote a book. He never held an office, never had a family or owned a house. He never went to college. He never traveled two hundred miles from the place where He was born.

He did none of the things one usually associates with greatness. He had no credentials, but Himself.

He was only thirty-three when the tide of public opinion turned against Him. His friends ran away. He was turned over to His enemies and went through the mockery of trial. He was nailed to a cross between two thieves. His executioners gambled for his clothing, the only property He had on earth. When He was dead He was laid in a borrowed grave. Twenty centuries have come and gone, and today Jesus is the central figure of the human race and the leader of mankind's progress.

All the armies that ever marched, all the navies that ever sailed, all the parliaments that have ever sat. All the kings that ever reigned put together, have not affected the life of mankind upon this earth as much as that ONE SOLITARY LIFE.

The power of his influence, the touch of his example, his effect on this world was incredible. And that's the real measure of a person. So, the real question for us to think about right now is: how do we measure up? In the scripture lesson, we are called to be "the light of the world." How are we doing? How bright is our light? What kind of example do we set? What do others do because of us? Are they happy or sad? Joyous or depressed? Lifted up or put down? Are they loving or hateful? Are they kind or cruel? Are they encouraged or discouraged? Are they in church or out of church?

Think about it: How do you measure up? How do you touch the lives of others? What is the power of your influence? Let's bring it close and be specific. How do you influence others at home, at church, in the world? Look quickly at those with me.

HOW DO YOU INFLUENCE OTHERS IN YOUR HOME?

What do you bring to your home? Do you bring light or darkness to others in your home? What do you cause other people in your family to do? to be happy? to be sad? to be kind or unkind? to be lifted up or depressed?

Paul Gilbert put it in a poem that goes like this:

You are writing a gospel, a chapter each day,

By deeds that you do, by words that you say.

Men read what you write, whether faithless or true,

Say, what is the gospel according to you?

What's the gospel according to you at home? Are you proud of your influence in your home?

Have you heard that poignant story about the little girl who had never heard the stories of Jesus because her parents had never taken her to church and had never told her about God? One day an uncle came for a visit. He was a committed Christian. He stayed with them for three days and at each meal he would say a prayer of thanksgiving to God. The little girl was fascinated by this. She watched her uncle pray and asked him about it. The uncle told her about God and about God's love. He told her the stories of Jesus, and he taught her how to pray. He taught her how to bow her head, and close her eyes, and put her little hands in front of her and say prayers of thanksgiving to God.

Finally his visit was over and the time came for the uncle to leave. The next morning, the little girl came to the breakfast table and scrambled up into her chair. She bowed her head, closed her eyes, put her hands in front of her, and waited for someone to say the prayer thanking God for a new day and the breakfast meal. But all she heard was the tinkling of the silverware and the crinkling of the morning paper as her mother and father rushed to get about the daily chores. The little girl was confused, and she looked up and said, "Mommy and Daddy, isn't there a God today?"

Can people tell by the way you live at home that there is indeed a God today in your life? You see, it's not just what we do; it is also what others do because of us.

HOW DO YOU INFLUENCE OTHERS AT CHURCH?

Some years ago, the telephone rang in my office. A young woman was calling to share with me something that was very important. "Jim, I just had to call to tell you what has happened to me in the last few months. A short time ago I was all mixed up. I read a lot of crazy things. I got confused, and I thought I was an atheist. But then I ran into a big problem that I couldn't handle. I reached out for God, but I didn't know how to find him. I had drifted so far away. I felt depressed, rejected, overwhelmed, alone, even a bit suicidal. But then, I decided to give the church one more chance. I realize now that it was not fair, but I was going to try the church one more time as a test, and I chose to come to your church. I walked in, and I found love, warmth, and acceptance—a community with open arms. They welcomed me. They brought me in."

Then she called the name of a lady who is devoted member of our church and said, "That neat, delightful woman with her warm smile and her genuine interest in me, her gracious acceptance of me and her unconditional love for me, saved my life. Now I'm a member of the church, I'm in Sunday school class. I'm coming to every service, and I'm loving every minute of it. And now I'm so glad to be alive."

Your influence at church is so important. How do you stack up? Are people coming into the church because of you? Do they find warmth and welcome here because of you? You see, it's not just what we do; it's also what others do because of us.

HOW DO YOU INFLUENCE OTHERS IN THE WORLD?

How do you influence others at work, at school, at social events, in casual conversations, or even in encounters with strangers? Are you the light of the world?

Some years ago, when we lived in Tennessee, I had a good friend named Bob. Bob was the head of the Salvation Army in that town. Bob had an amazing story to tell about his life. He would go out to churches and schools and youth groups and civic meetings to tell his personal story, and it was remarkable.

Seventeen years earlier, Bob showed up at the Salvation Army in Tennessee. He didn't know how he had gotten there! The last thing he remembered was that he was in a bar in the state of Ohio. You see, Bob was an alcoholic. At the time, he had been drunk for more than a month. Somehow in his drunken stupor, he had made his way from Ohio to Tennessee, and he was now knocking on the door of the Salvation Army. He had not eaten or showered or changed his clothes or brushed his teeth for more than a month. He had just been drinking whiskey. His eyes were bloodshot, and his clothes were filthy. He looked horrible and smelled worse. A wonderful, kind, gracious man in a Salvation Army uniform answered Bob's knock at the door. He looked at Bob and then said words that would change Bob's life forever. He said, "May I help you, Sir?" Bob said, "That was a crowning moment for me because that Christlike man did not say, 'What do you want?' He did not say, 'You look terrible and smell awful.' He said, 'May I help you, *Sir*?'"

Bob said, "I could not believe my ears. He called me SIR." How long had it been since anyone called me Sir? And in that moment," Bob said, "I made up mind to call out to God for help, to ask God to save me and to cleanse me and to redeem me and to turn my life around. That kind man called me Sir! He treated me with love and respect, and it made all the difference!"

Now, where did that man in the Salvation Army uniform learn to do that? to treat all people with love and respect and kindness? You know, don't you? The same place we learn it: at home, at church, but most of all, from Jesus!

Jesus taught us that the best way to show our love for God is to show love for all of his children. Look what the miracle of love did for Bob. The Salvation Army took him in that night. They gave him food and a shower and a bed and a job. The next day Bob went to work as an assistant cook in the Salvation Army kitchen, and by the grace of God, five years later, he became the executive director of the Salvation Army—and all because of that *Kairos* moment seventeen years before when a man answering the door treated him with love, respect, compassion, and kindness, a man who had the grace to say, "May I help you, Sir?"

This is our calling as Christians, isn't it? To be a light to the world! To share the light of God's unconditional love with everyone we meet.

FOUR

What Can We Learn From Our Children?

Luke 18:15-17

Some months ago I was invited to give a lecture series in a church in another state. I arrived early and went directly into the sanctuary to see the lay of the land—to see where I would sit, to get the feel of the pulpit, and to check out the sound system. While I was looking around, a teacher brought a group of young children into the sanctuary to show them the faith symbols in that sacred room. She showed them the pulpit, the choir loft, the organ, the worship center, the communion rail, the baptismal font, and then she told them she had a special "surprise" for them.

"I want to show you my favorite stained glass window," she said. She led her class over to the second window from the front on the right-hand side. It depicted a youthful angelic figure. Then the teacher said: "Now, boys and girls, this is the Ida Lee Chapman window. When she was nine years old, Ida Lee Chapman gave the first dollar toward the building of this sanctuary where we now worship. Listen closely…" the teacher said, "and I will tell you her story." The children were "all ears" and so was I.

"It was a Sunday morning in 1911," she said. The church was packed, so much so that some people had to stand up against the wall in the back. The minister, taking note of the large crowd, pointed out that the congregation had simply outgrown the church building and that before long a drive for funds would have to be launched so they could build a new and larger sanctuary. After the service was over, little nine-year-old Ida Lee Chapman came down to speak to the minister. She dug deep down into her Sunday purse and pulled out a silver dollar. She told the minister that she had been saving that silver dollar for a long time for a very special occasion: to buy something very special and very valuable.

She then gave the silver dollar to the minister for the new church building. Ida Lee Chapman's gracious gift became the first gift toward the building of the new sanctuary, and the next Sunday when the minister told that story, her gesture became the inspiration the congregation needed in order to raise the money to construct that beautiful place of worship, which has served so many people since its completion in 1913.

Strangely and tragically, two weeks after Ida Lee's gift was made, she became ill and quite suddenly and quite unexpectedly died. The church members were so touched by her faith and witness and generosity, and so saddened by her death, that they gave that stained glass window in her memory, and it was the first one installed.

Seventy-five years later, when the cornerstone was opened, what do you think they found? A number of treasured items that symbolized the faith, the heritage, and the spirit of that church—and yes, one of those treasured items was Ida Lee Chapman's silver dollar and the story of her gracious and inspiring faith. Underneath the center panel of that stained glass window are two inscriptions: (1) "In memory of Ida Lee Chapman"; (2) "And a little child shall lead them." (Isaiah)

Isn't that a great verse? "A little child shall lead them." Jesus knew that verse well. He must have had it in mind that day when he said: "Let the children come to me, and do not hinder them, for the kingdom of God belongs to such as these." And he added: "Truly I tell you" (by the way, that means, "Get ready! This is supremely important!") "anyone who will not receive the kingdom of God like a child will never enter it" (Mark 10:13-16 NIV).

It's so true, isn't it? We can learn so much from our children. They have so much to teach us. Think of it: perfect trust, wide-eyed wonder, eager expectancy, lack of pretense, delightful and uninhibited laughter, unconditional love—these are just a few of the great lessons we can learn from our children, and I'm sure that these were some of the qualities Jesus had in mind that day. With that in mind, let me list for our consideration some other very valuable truths our children can teach us if we will stop long enough to look and listen and learn.

OUR CHILDREN CAN TEACH US THE IMPORTANCE OF CELEBRATING THE DIFFERENT STAGES OF LIFE

An important key to living is to realize that life is a series of stages and that each stage is tremendously important. We move from one stage to another, not just through childhood and youth but all through life, and each stage has a unique contribution to make toward the full and proper development of a personality. When we get into trouble is when we try to skip stages or grow up too fast.

If I may paraphrase the writer of Ecclesiastes in the Old Testament:

> God has made everything beautiful in its own time. For everything there is a season and a stage.
>
> There is a time for a teething ring and a time for an infant seat.

There is a time for crawling and a time for toddling

There is a time for puppy love and a time for baseball.

There is a time for love letters and a time for telephone calls.

There is a time for a drivers' license and a time for slumber parties.

There is a time for family togetherness and a time for personal privacy.

There is a time to discuss and a time to think.

There is a time to date and a time to take on more responsibilities.

There is a time to study and prepare and a time to get married.

There is a time to get a job and a time to retire.

On and on life goes, and each one of these stages is important. If we miss one or skip one or even abbreviate one, we miss something of life. Let me illustrate that rather dramatically.

Some years ago, when we were living in another state, there was a most unusual little girl in our congregation. Never before or since have I heard of a child doing what she did. She was remarkably bright, and she had this intense desire to learn how to talk, so much so that she gave all of her creative energy to the task of learning to talk. The result was that by the time she was nearly two, she could speak as fluently as an adult, but she could not walk.

She had never taken a single step. She had never tried to walk. She had never tried to crawl. Physically, she was able to walk, but she had given so much effort to talking that she had missed out on crawling and walking. It was the strangest thing to hear this little child say: "Mommy, will you please take me over to the couch?" or "Daddy, would you please take me into the den so I can watch television? There is a superb program on at this hour."

Of course, eventually she decided that she wanted to walk and she learned quickly. But here was the problem: she skipped the crawling stage! She went from having somebody carry her about to walking on her own and the consequence was that she now has eye problems that she will have for the rest of her life because she missed the eye-focusing development that comes to babies during the crawling stage.

It is physically true that we best "crawl before we

walk." But it is true in more ways than just that one. In fact, much of the heartache you see in the counseling room comes from "stage-skipping." *He had too much too soon. She grew up too fast. They weren't really ready for marriage.* You see, God has a wonderful plan for us: a life that develops in significant stages, each one important, each one valid, each one vital, each one valuable.

If we will stop, look, and listen long enough, our children will teach us the critical lesson of celebrating the stages of life. God has made every stage beautiful in its own time.

OUR CHILDREN CAN TEACH US THE IMPORTANCE OF FORGIVENESS

Children have so many amazing qualities, but I think one of the most important of all is their wonderful ability to forgive and forget.

When our son was about nine or ten years old, he went to the circus with some friends of ours. We gave him fifteen dollars to buy his ticket and have a little left over for food and souvenirs. What we didn't know was that our friends had already bought his ticket. So, he spent all the money on food—hot dogs,

Cracker Jacks, popcorn, pretzels, cotton candy, peanuts, soft drinks. (You could buy lots more for fiftenn dollars then, and he spent it all!)

I had been up most of the night before in a crisis at the hospital and was very tired. So, when our son returned from his "eating binge" at the circus and then got sick at 1:00 a.m., I became (how shall I say this?) very "parental." "Didn't you know better than to eat all that junk? Didn't you know that would make you sick? What were you thinking about?"

Our nine-year-old boy reached over and gently patted me on my arm and said, "I'm sorry, Daddy." Well, that melted me. That brought me back to my senses, and I began to apologize to him for my impatience. He patted my arm again and said, "It's OK, Dad. It's OK." Pretty soon, he was back to sleep. I went to bed feeling guilty, and I could hardly wait until morning to apologize again. "Son, I'm so sorry that you were sick last night, and I'm so sorry that I was so impatient with you. Will you please forgive me?" Do you know what? He didn't even remember it. He had already forgiven me. He had forgotten it. He had put it behind him. That is a beautiful quality, indeed a Godlike quality.

A few years ago, rumors spread that a certain woman was having visions of Jesus. The word reached the archbishop, and he decided to check her out. "Is it true, ma'am, that you have visions of Jesus?" asked the archbishop. "Yes," the woman replied.

"Does he talk to you in the visions?"

"Oh, yes," the woman answered.

"Well," said the archbishop, "the next time you have a vision, I want you to ask Jesus to tell you the sins that I confessed in my last confession. Please call me if anything happens." A few days later the woman notified the archbishop that she had indeed had another vision and visit with Jesus. The archbishop said, "What did Jesus say? Did he tell you what sins I confessed in my last confession?"

The woman took the archbishop's hand, gazed deep into his eyes, and said, "We did talk about that. I did ask him and these were his exact words. He said, 'I don't remember!'"

The importance of forgiving and forgetting: that's another great and Godlike lesson we can learn from our children.

OUR CHILDREN CAN TEACH US THE IMPORTANCE OF RELATIONSHIPS

Material things are nice, but they don't last, they don't satisfy, they don't fulfill, they don't really bring enduring happiness. The key to life is found not in "things," but in healthy relationships. Show me a person who has a good relationship with God, a good relationship with others, and a good relationship with self (a healthy self-esteem), and I will show you a happy, productive, fulfilled person.

Some second graders were learning about magnets in a science class one morning. The children were shown how small nails, paper clips, and bobby pins were drawn to the magnet. Later, the teacher gave a test on the material and asked this question: "What has six letters, starts with 'M' and picks things up?" Of course, the answer she was looking for was "magnet." However, more than half the class answered "mother"!

Well, good moms and dads not only "pick things up," they also lift people up! There is way too much "put down" in our world these days. We in the church and we in the Christian home need to work overtime in lifting people up.

It is great to give our children nice things, but it is infinitely better to give them love and respect. It is nice to give our children the riches of the world, but much, much better to give them the riches of the soul. The best thing we can do for them is to love them unconditionally and to help them have good relationships with God and other people. We are what we are by our relationships, and when we are at peace with ourselves and at peace with others, we are more likely to be at peace with God. Actually, that is better put the other way around: being at peace with God enables us to be at peace with ourselves and with others. Jesus talked about this a lot. He said the greatest righteousness is to be rightly related to God and rightly related to others! So, let there be peace on earth and let it begin at home where we intentionally encourage a healthy self-esteem, a healthy love for others, and a healthy love for God.

The point is clear: the key to meaningful life is not found in "things" but in "loving relationships." This is what Jesus taught long ago, and that's what we can learn from our children every day.

There is a powerful line in the play *Nicholas Nickleby* that underscores this great truth dramatically. The hero, Nicholas Nickleby, has rescued and befriended an afflicted boy named Smike. Smike has had a tough life. At so young an age, he has been the victim of heartbreaking cruelty. But Nicholas Nickleby befriends him and takes care of him and treats him with respect and love and in essence adopts him as his own.

They are trying to decide where to live, where to make their home. Nicholas lays out the possibilities, but the boy, Smike, is not interested in the relative merits of place. Smike doesn't really care where they end up, as long as they are together.

Struggling to find a way to express this, young Smike turns to Nicholas at last and says simply, "Nicholas, you are my home! Home is with you. Home is where you are. It doesn't matter to me where we are as long as you are there."

On a deeper theological level, this is what the Psalm writer meant when he wrote, "As the deer pants for streams of water, / so my soul pants for you, O God" (Psalm 42:1 NIV). And this is what the great Christian Augustine meant when he said, "My soul is restless, O God, 'til it finds its rest in Thee."

Be honest now: are you at home with God? Have you come home to him? Are you in right relationship with your Lord? You can count on it. Your soul will be restless 'til it finds its rest in him. Nothing else can satisfy. Nothing else will work. Nothing else can do it. Nothing else can fulfill—only a right relationship with God.

What can we learn from our children? So many things: the importance of celebrating all the wonderful stages of life, the importance of forgiveness, and the importance of relationships.